—— Words of ——
LIFE

My Precious Friend
Esther:

I love you, and
you have been greatly
on my mind.
Know that I love you
and Care, when you hurt.
Ever and Always your
friend: Chloetta

Words of
LIFE

Thomas Nelson Publishers
Nashville • Camden • New York

THE WORD OF LIFE

Before the world was created, the Word already
existed; he was with God, and he was the same
as God. From the very beginning the Word was
with God.
Through him God made all things; not one thing
in all creation was made without him.
The Word was the source of life, and this life
brought light to mankind. The light shines in the
darkness, and the darkness has never put it out.

JOHN 1:1–5

"GOD MADE THEM ALL"

God commanded,
"Let the water be filled with many kinds of living beings, and let the air be filled with birds." So God created the great sea monsters, all kinds of creatures that live in the water, and all kinds of birds.

And God was pleased with what he saw. He blessed them all and told the creatures that live in the water to reproduce and to fill the sea, and he told the birds to increase in number. Evening passed and morning came—that was the fifth day.

Then God commanded,
"Let the earth produce all kinds of animal life: domestic and wild, large and small"—and it was done. So God made them all, and he was pleased with what he saw.

GENESIS 1:20–25

THE GARDEN

The Lord God took some soil from the ground and formed a man out of it; he breathed life-giving breath into his nostrils and the man began to live.

Then the Lord God planted a garden in Eden, in the East, and there he put the man he had formed. He made all kinds of beautiful trees grow there and produce good fruit. In the middle of the garden stood the tree that gives life and the tree that gives knowledge of what is good and what is bad.

GENESIS 2:7–9

CREATURES LARGE AND SMALL

Lord, you have made so many things!
How wisely you made them all!
The earth is filled with your creatures.
There is the ocean, large and wide,
where countless creatures live,
large and small alike.
The ships sail on it,
and in it plays Leviathan,
that sea monster which you made.
All of them depend on you
to give them food when they need it.
You give it to them, and they eat it;
you provide food and they are satisfied.
When you turn away, they are afraid;
when you take away their breath, they die and
go back to the dust from which they came.
But when you give them breath, they are created;
you give new life to the earth.

PSALM 104:24–30

CHOOSE LIFE

Moses said:
"Today I am giving you a choice between good
and evil, between life and death.

If you obey the commands of the Lord your God,
which I give you today, if you love him, obey
him, and keep all his laws, then you will prosper
and become a nation of many people. The Lord
your God will bless you in the land that you are
about to occupy.

But if you disobey and refuse to listen, and are
led away to worship other gods, you will be
destroyed—I warn you here and now.
You will not live long in that land across the
Jordan that you are about to occupy.

I am now giving you the choice between life and
death, between God's blessing and God's curse,
and I call heaven and earth to witness the choice
you make.
Choose life."

DEUTERONOMY 30:15–19

"LIKE THE SUNRISE"

The road the righteous travel is like the sunrise, getting brighter and brighter until daylight has come. The road of the wicked, however, is dark as night. They fall, but cannot see what they have stumbled over.

Son, pay attention to what I say. Listen to my words. Never let them get away from you. Remember them and keep them in your heart. They will give life and health to anyone who understands them. Be careful how you think; your life is shaped by your thoughts.

PROVERBS 4:18–23

THE WAY

Jesus said:
"I am the way, the truth, and the life;
no one goes to the Father except by me."

JOHN 14:6

LIFE IN ALL ITS FULLNESS

Jesus said again,
"I am telling you the truth: I am the gate for the sheep. All others who came before me are thieves and robbers, but the sheep did not listen to them. I am the gate. Whoever comes in by me will be saved; he will come in and go out and find pasture. The thief comes only in order to steal, kill and destroy. I have come in order that you might have life—life in all its fullness."

JOHN 10:7–10

"A NEW BEING"

When anyone is joined to Christ, he is a new
being; the old is gone, the new has come.
All this is done by God, who through Christ
changed us from enemies into his friends . . .

2 CORINTHIANS 5:17–18

"I WILL LIVE FOR YOU"

Lord, I will live for you, for you alone;
Heal me and let me live.
My bitterness will turn into peace.
You save my life from all danger;
You forgive all my sins.
No one in the world of the dead can praise you;
The dead cannot trust in your faithfulness.
It is the living who praise you,
As I praise you now.
Fathers tell their children how faithful you are.
Lord, you have healed me.
We will play harps and sing your praise,
Sing praise in your Temple as long as we live.

ISAIAH 38:16–20

"THE WAY IS HARD"

Jesus said:
"The gate to life is narrow and the way that leads to it is hard, and there are few people who find it."

MATTHEW 7:14

Once a man came to Jesus. "Teacher," he asked, "what good thing must I do to receive eternal life?"

"Why do you ask me concerning what is good?" answered Jesus. "There is only One who is good. Keep the commandments if you want to enter life."

"What commandments?" he asked.

Jesus answered, "Do not commit murder; do not commit adultery; do not steal; do not accuse anyone falsely; respect your father and your mother; and love your neighbor as you love yourself."

"I have obeyed all these commandments," the young man replied. "What else do I need to do?"

Jesus said to him, "If you want to be perfect, go and sell all you have and give the money to the poor, and you will have riches in heaven; then come and follow me."

When the young man heard this, he went away sad, because he was very rich.

MATTHEW 19:16–22

LOSING AND GAINING

Jesus said:
"Whoever loves his father or mother more than me is not fit to be my disciple; whoever loves his son or daughter more than me is not fit to be my disciple. Whoever does not take up his cross and follow in my steps is not fit to be my disciple. Whoever tries to gain his own life will lose it; but whoever loses his life for my sake will gain it."

MATTHEW 10:37–39

NOT DEATH, BUT LIFE

Jesus said:
"God loved the world so much that he gave his only Son, so that everyone who believes in him may not die but have eternal life. For God did not send his Son into the world to be its judge, but to be its savior."

JOHN 3:16–17

THE SOURCE OF LIFE

Jesus said:
"I am telling you the truth: whoever hears my words and believes in him who sent me has eternal life. He will not be judged, but has already passed from death to life. I am telling you the truth: the time is coming—the time has already come—when the dead will hear the voice of the Son of God, and those who hear it will come to life. Just as the Father is himself the source of life, in the same way he has made his Son to be the source of life. And he has given the Son the right to judge, because he is the Son of Man."

JOHN 5:24–27

NEVER HUNGRY

Jesus said:
"I am the bread of life. He who comes to me will never be hungry; he who believes in me will never be thirsty. Now, I told you that you have seen me but will not believe. Everyone whom my Father gives me will come to me. I will never turn away anyone who comes to me, because I have come down from heaven to do not my own will but the will of him who sent me. And it is the will of him who sent me that I should not lose any of all those he has given me, but that I should raise them all to life on the last day. For what my Father wants is that all who see the Son and believe in him should have eternal life. And I will raise them to life on the last day."

JOHN 6:35–40

LIFE-GIVING WATER

Jesus said:
"Whoever drinks this water will get thirsty again,
but whoever drinks the water that I will give him
will never be thirsty again. The water that I will
give him will become in him a spring which will
provide him with life-giving water and give him
eternal life."

JOHN 4:13–14

"I AM THE LIFE"

Jesus said:
"I am the resurrection and the life. Whoever believes in me will live, even though he dies; and whoever lives and believes in me will never die. Do you believe this?"

JOHN 11:25–26

REAL LIFE

You have been raised to life with Christ, so set
your hearts on the things that are in heaven,
where Christ sits on his throne at the right side
of God. Keep your minds fixed on things there,
not on things here on earth. For you have died,
and your life is hidden with Christ in God. Your
real life is Christ and when he appears, then you
too will appear with him and share his glory!

COLOSSIANS 3:1–4

LIFE AND JOY

We write to you about the Word of life, which
has existed from the very beginning. We have
heard it, and we have seen it with our eyes; yes,
we have seen it, and our hands have touched it.
When this life became visible, we saw it; so we
speak of it and tell you about the eternal life
which was with the Father and was made known
to us. What we have seen and heard we
announce to you also, so that you will join with
us in the fellowship that we have with the Father
and with his Son Jesus Christ. We write this in
order that our joy may be complete.

1 JOHN 1:1–4